TRAVEL WITH THE GREAT EXPLORERS

Explore with
Marco Polo

Tim Cooke

Crabtree Publishing Company
www.crabtreebooks.com

Crabtree Publishing Company
www.crabtreebooks.com

Author: Tim Cooke
Publishing plan research
  and development: Reagan Miller
Editors: Kathy Middleton, Shannon Welbourn
Designer: Lynne Lennon
Picture Manager: Sophie Mortimer
Design Manager: Keith Davis
Editorial Director: Lindsey Lowe
Children's Publisher: Anne O'Daly
Production coordinator
  and prepress technician: Tammy McGarr
Print coordinator: Katherine Berti

Produced by Brown Bear Books for
Crabtree Publishing Company

Photographs:
Front Cover: Corbis: The Gallery Collection main; Shutterstock: Aleksander Hunta tr, M. Unai Ozmen br; Thinkstock: istockphoto cr.

Interior: British Museum: 18; Dreamstime: 15tr, 17bl, 22b; istockphoto: 4t, 22t; Metropolitan Museum of Art: 19t; Public Domain: 17t, 24b, Abraham Cresques, Atlas Catalan 12; Robert Hunt Library: 29t, Le Livre des Merveilles 29b; Shutterstock: 16, 20, 21t, 25b, Ekaterina Fribus 14b, Aleksander Hunta 17c, Katalin Kiszaly 23t, Megula 4b, Travellight 7b, Archvadze Paata 13b, Julia Reese 25c: Thinkstock: AbleStock 27b, Dorling Kindersley RF 5, Hemera 25tr, istockphoto 10, 13t, 15bl, 19b, 23b, 24t, 25tc, 26, 27t, 28tl, 28b, Photos.com6, Photodisc 7t.

All other artwork and maps, Brown Bear Books.

Brown Bear Books has made every attempt to contact the copyright holder. If you have any information please contact licensing@brownbearbooks.co.uk

Library and Archives Canada Cataloguing in Publication

Cooke, Tim, 1961-, author
     Explore with Marco Polo / Tim Cooke.

(Travel with the great explorers)
Includes index.
Issued in print and electronic formats.
ISBN 978-0-7787-1428-6 (bound).--ISBN 978-0-7787-1434-7 (pbk.).--
ISBN 978-1-4271-7585-4 (pdf).--ISBN 978-1-4271-7579-3 (html)

     1. Polo, Marco, 1254-1323?--Juvenile literature. 2. Travelers--
Italy--Biography--Juvenile literature. 3. Travelers--China--
Biography--Juvenile literature. 4. Merchants--Italy--Venice--
Biography--Juvenile literature. 5. China--Description and travel--
Juvenile literature. 6. Asia--Description and travel--Juvenile
literature. 7. Travel, Medieval--Juvenile literature. 8. Mongols--
History--Juvenile literature. I. Title.

G370.P9C66 2014   j915.0422092   C2014-903662-0
                                               C2014-903663-9

Library of Congress Cataloging-in-Publication Data

Cooke, Tim, 1961-
 Explore with Marco Polo / Tim Cooke.
   pages cm. -- (Travel with the great explorers)
 Includes index.
 ISBN 978-0-7787-1428-6 (reinforced library binding) --
 ISBN 978-0-7787-1434-7 (pbk.) --
 ISBN 978-1-4271-7585-4 (electronic pdf) --
 ISBN 978-1-4271-7579-3 (electronic html)
 1. Polo, Marco, 1254-1323?--Juvenile literature. 2. Asia--Description
and travel--Juvenile literature. 3. Voyages and travels--Juvenile
literature. I. Title.

 G370.P9C67 2015
 910.4--dc23
                         2014020431

Crabtree Publishing Company

www.crabtreebooks.com   1-800-387-7650

Printed in Hong Kong/082014/BK20140613

Published in Canada
Crabtree Publishing
616 Welland Ave.
St. Catharines, ON
L2M 5V6

Published in the United States
Crabtree Publishing
PMB 59051
350 Fifth Avenue, 59th Floor
New York, New York 10118

Published in the United Kingdom
Crabtree Publishing
Maritime House
Basin Road North, Hove
BN41 1WR

Published in Australia
Crabtree Publishing
3 Charles Street
Coburg North
VIC, 3058

CONTENTS

Meet the Boss

Marco Polo was an Italian explorer who traveled to Asia. The emperor of China, Kublai Khan, was so impressed by him, he asked Polo to work for him. Back home, the stories of his travels made Polo famous.

YOUNG HERO DOES NOT TRAVEL ALONE

+ Great author never went to school—shocking claim!

Marco Polo was born in Italy in 1254. He traveled to Asia at age 17 with his father, Niccolo, and his uncle, Maffeo. They were **merchants** from Venice. When Marco was born, Niccolo was away trading in Asia. While he was gone, his wife, Marco's mother, died. Young Marco did not go to school, but he learned to read and write. Some experts think he spent time at the docks, listening to sailors' stories of distant places.

TRAVEL UPDATE

Venice for Visitors
★ Welcome to the most important port on the Mediterranean Sea! In the 1200s, Venice was a vital link between Asia and Europe. Merchants sailed to both Southwest Asia and Northeast Africa. Slaves from Russia, Africa, and Turkey were brought there to be sold. Venice grew wealthy from all the trade.

LOCAL MAN GETS TOP JOB

★ **Works for powerful emperor**

★ **Travels widely**

In Asia, Marco met Kublai Kahn, the Mongol emperor of China. The Polos joined Kublai Khan's court. Marco served the emperor for 17 years. As the Khan's ambassador, or representative, Polo visited many parts of Asia, including China, India, and Persia (now Iran). He saw things no European had ever seen before. His tales of the gold, silks, and **spices** he found inspired other explorers to travel to Asia.

BOOK REVIEW

☞ **Can this really be true?**

Polo's book, *The Description of the World*, was published in 1298. It described his adventures in Asia. The book was a bestseller, because it described things Europeans knew nothing about. But many readers did not believe Polo's stories. They called the book *Il Millione* (The Million), because they said it contained a million lies.

> They have plenty of **unicorns**, which are scarcely smaller than elephants. They have the hair of a buffalo and feet like an elephant's. They have a single large, black horn in the middle of the forehead."
> *Marco Polo describes unicorns in Asia*

My Explorer Journal

★ **Imagine that you are the 17-year-old Marco Polo. Your father and uncle are setting out to travel to China. Write a letter to your father Niccolo explaining why you think you should go along on the journey.**

Where Are We Heading?

Marco Polo's travels with his father and uncle took him eastward to China. While he was working for Kublai Khan, Marco became one of the first Europeans to see many places in Asia still famous today.

ESCAPE FROM THE CITY!

- Travelers head into wilderness
- Leave Venice behind

When they left Venice, the Polos headed through the Mediterranean to Acre, in what is now Israel. They traveled through Anatolia (now Turkey) and then to the Persian Gulf before entering Persia. From there they had to cross Central Asia to reach China, then called Cathay.

Weather Forecast

PACK FOR ALL WEATHERS!

The Polos experienced all kinds of extreme weather. In the desert they faced boiling-hot days and huge wind-whipped sandstorms. At night and in the high mountains, it was freezing cold, and the travelers had to light big campfires and put on all their clothes to keep warm.

EUROPE'S WORST ENEMIES

★ **Raiders from the East**

★ **Who are the Mongols?**

The Mongols came from Mongolia, north of China. They were called Tartars by the Europeans, who said they came from Tartarus, or Hell. In 1206 the Mongol ruler, Genghis Khan, conquered China and **raided** other lands as far as Europe. When Kublai became Khan, or ruler, in 1260, the Mongol empire covered most of Asia and eastern Europe.

ALL ROADS LEAD TO RICHES

+ Trade goes global

Mongol rulers encouraged trade. Merchants traveled safely along the Silk Road, a series of routes throughout Asia. Following the Silk Road, Europeans obtained spices, perfumes, silks, cotton, and pearls from as far away as China.

TRAVEL UPDATE

Slow Voyage by Sea!

★ At the end of their adventure, it took the Polos two years to sail to Persia with a fleet of 14 ships. They escorted a Mongol princess to her new husband. When the news came that Kublai Khan had died, they headed for home, finally returning to Venice in 1295.

Marco Polo's Travels in Asia

On the way to China, Marco Polo and his companions traveled along an overland route called the Silk Road. On their way home many years later, they sailed around Southeast Asia and across the Indian Ocean.

Venice

Marco Polo and his father and uncle left Venice in 1271. They did not return for another 17 years. At the time, Venice was one of the most important trading cities in Europe.

Italy

Anatolia

Pers

Hormuz

The Polos intended to sail from the port of Hormuz on the Persian Gulf to India. But when Polo saw the boats the Persians used, he was worried that they would sink. Instead, the Polos decided to stay on land and follow the Silk Road through the heart of Asia.

AFRICA

Pamirs

These high, grassy plains were one of the coldest parts of the journey. They lay in the middle of some of the tallest mountains in the world. Polo said that no birds could fly here because the air was so thin.

Jerusalem

The Polos' first destination was Jerusalem. They had to collect holy oil to give to Kublai Khan as a gift from Pope Gregory X, the head of the Catholic Church.

Taklamakan

Crossing the desert was one of the most difficult parts of the journey. It took over a month. Polo claimed that evil spirits called men's names to make them turn off the route, and that the men who ventured off were never found again.

Shangdu

The Polos visited Kublai Khan in his summer palace at Shangdu. It became famous in Europe for its great luxury. Europeans called it "Xanadu."

Sumatra

In 1292 the Polos left Kublai Khan to go on a mission to take a Mongol princess to Persia to be married. The voyage took two years, and many of the nearly 600 people who set out did not survive.

Russia

ASIA

Mongolia

China

India

Locator map

Key

· · · · · ▶ **Outward journey**

– – – ▶ **Return journey**

Meet the Crew

When Marco Polo's father and uncle decided to return across Asia to visit Kublai Khan, they came into contact with many people – including some of the most powerful people of the age.

TRAVEL UPDATE

Local Merchants With Big Plans!

★ Niccolo and Maffeo Polo first left Venice, Italy, in 1253, just before Marco was born. They sailed to Constantinople, in Turkey, where they spent six years. Then they sailed to Uzbekistan. When a war broke out, they stayed there three more years.

MEET THE GREAT KHAN!

Kublai Kahn ruled the great Mongol empire. When his ambassador in Uzbekistan met Niccolo and Maffeo Polo in 1260, the Khan wanted to meet the merchants from Venice. The Polo brothers crossed the desert and visited Kublai Khan's palace in present-day Beijing, China. Kublai asked the Polos to describe Europe's different countries and rulers. When it was time for the Polos to leave, Kublai made them promise to return.

A NEW POPE

★ **Gregory X takes charge!**

Niccolo and Maffeo got home in 1269 after a three-year journey from China. They passed on Kublai's request to meet representatives of the Pope, Europe's religious ruler. After waiting two years for a new pope to be elected, their friend Teobaldo was chosen and named Gregory X. In 1271, Gregory allowed the Polos to visit Jerusalem. They collected some holy oil to give to the Khan as a gift from the Pope.

> "They were the most learned and worthy [men] that were in all that province."
> *Marco Polo describes the Pope's friars.*

FRIGHTENED FRIARS

☛ **Papal ambassadors run away**

☛ **Scared off by bandits**

Kublai Khan had asked the Pope to send 100 priests to teach the Mongols about Christianity. But Gregory X would not send so many people this distance. He sent just two **friars** with Niccolo and Maffeo. This time Marco got to go. But when they got to what is now Turkey, their **caravan** was attacked by bandits. While the Polos carried on, the two friars went home.

Attack

When bandits attacked the caravan in which the Polos and the friars were traveling, they killed many of the merchants. The Polos hid in a local village.

My Explorer Journal

★ Imagine you are one of the friars who ran away while crossing the desert. Write a letter to the Pope giving some reasons why you gave up on the journey.

Check Out the Ride

In Marco Polo's time, travel was slow, especially over land. Not everyone could afford horses, so even long journeys were made on foot. It was usually far quicker to travel by sea.

CAMEL CARAVAN

☛ Let's form a convoy!

☛ Safety in numbers

To cross deserts or empty land, merchants often formed caravans. They gathered in a town before setting off with the camels and horses that carried their goods. At night they set up camps. There was enough of them to help guard one another from bandits.

BY GOLLY, IT'S A GALLEY

+ Ship used for warfare or trade

Historians are not sure what type of ship the Polos used to sail home to Italy from Asia. Some believe they sailed in a large, fast ship called a galley. Galleys were long and narrow and were usually powered by oars, although they also had sails. During the **Middle Ages**, galleys were armed with weapons and used as warships. They were also used by merchants to carry goods to trade in other countries.

WHAT A LOAD OF JUNK

★ **Cutting-edge Chinese technology**

★ **Are junks better than European ships?**

When they sailed on behalf of Kublai Khan, the Polos used Chinese ships called **junks**. They varied in size, but some of them were larger than any European ships of the period. They often had large raised sections at the front and the back to store cargo. There were covered living quarters for the crew, who sometimes lived onboard permanently. Junks were powered by sails made of bamboo. The Mongols benefited from Chinese ship-building technology. They used junks to launch invasions of both Japan and the island of Java.

TRAVEL UPDATE

Going Native!

★ When the Polos crossed the Indian Ocean, they hired local **pilots**. These expert seamen knew how to use the monsoon winds to their advantage. The winds changed regularly, so knowing where to find them and which direction they were blowing in could make for a much shorter voyage.

Solve It With Science

Done!

Science in Marco Polo's time was not about theories or ideas. It was about coming up with actual solutions to problems, such as how to find your way.

All travelers relied on science to find their way. They used astronomy and maps to navigate, or find their way. When the Polos reached China, they discovered that Asia had its own forms of science.

DEAD RECKONING

- Cloudy day? No worries!

- Easy as falling off a log

Sailors figured out the position of their ship by measuring how far it had sailed from a known point. They used ropes tied with knots to measure their speed. The rope was tied to a log and dropped into the water. Then sailors measured how much rope had been pulled into the water over a certain time. That told them how fast they were sailing, measured by the number of knots.

WHERE ARE WE?
★ It's all in the stars

The Polos navigated by using a device called an **astrolabe**. The astrolabe measured how high the sun or stars appeared above the horizon. By comparing this to the ship's course, or path, sailors were able to figure out where they were. Judging a ship's position based on the sun or the stars is called celestial navigation.

BOLD CLAIMS

★ **Umm, are you sure?**

★ **Experts doubt claims**

At that time, one key branch of science was military science. Polo wrote that they taught Kublai how to build **mangonels**, which are like huge catapults. He said the Mongols used the weapons to capture a city—but modern experts say the city fell two years before the Polos even arrived in Asia.

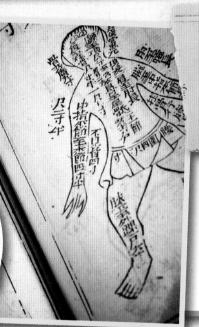

ASIAN SCIENCE

☞ **Wonders of medicine**

☞ **Curing pain with pins!**

The Polos were fascinated by Asian medicine. For thousands of years the Chinese had been using herbs to cure illnesses. They also used acupuncture. Doctors put tiny pins in the skin to help cure people of diseases.

Did you know?

Explorers used to drop a piece of lead tied to a piece of rope overboard to measure the depth of the sea.

THE QUADRANT

+ Figuring out north or south

Sailors could figure out how far north or south a ship was using a **quadrant**. One arm of the quadrant pointed at the horizon and the other at the sun. The greater the angle between the arms, the further a ship was from the **equator**.

Hanging at Home

The Polos were away from home for decades. While they worked for Kublai Khan they lived in luxury. But their travels took them to places where there were few comforts—and sometimes danger.

Did you know?

Between the Pamir Mountains and the Taklamakan Desert, the Polos stayed at the town of Khot on the Silk Road. Khotan is farth from the ocean than nearly any other place in the world.

Weather Forecast

SURVIVING IN THE PAMIRS

The Pamirs are mostly grazing land on the tallest mountains in the world, including the Himalayas. The air has so little oxygen, fires cannot burn easily. The Polos were often cold and were barely able to cook their food.

THE KHAN'S COURT

★ **Food fit for a king**

★ **A welcome feast for the Polos**

When the Polos finally reached Cambulac (Beijing), they were taken to Kublai Khan's palace. The Khan was pleased to see them and held a feast in their honor. He was excited about the gift of holy oil from the Pope. Among the other Asian foods Polo tried were rhubarb and horse's milk.

TRAVEL UPDATE

Highs and Lows

★ The Polos' journey took them through extreme landscapes. The Pamirs were lush green pastures. Their next destination, the Desert of Lop, was gravel and sand that went on for hundreds of miles. Polo said that travelers had to carry a month's food and water to survive.

> " There dwell many spirits that make for wayfarers great and wonderful illusions to make them perish."
>
> *Polo describes how travelers get lost in the desert.*

AT HOME WITH THE MONGOLS

☛ **World's greatest horsemen**

☛ **Life in a yurt**

The Mongols were **nomads** who came from the steppes, or grasslands, of Mongolia, where they bred horses. They were famous horsemen. They lived in **yurts**. These round tents were made of horse skins and were easy to take down and move to a new location.

Meeting and Greeting

Marco Polo and his companions met all kinds of people as they traveled. Most of them were friendly and helped the Polos, but some were hostile. Polo wrote about their encounters.

Did you know?

Marco Polo wrote lots of stories about the wealthy cities of Persia. But his account does not say whether he actually visited them all.

SILENCE

☛ **Don't speak during deals!**

☛ **Merchants trade secretly**

In Tabriz on the Persian Gulf, the Polos met pearl sellers. The sellers made private deals by holding hands with the buyer. Their hands were covered with fabric. They negotiated by squeezing each other's fingers and wrists.

THE PLEASURES OF PERSIA

★ **Learning and luxury**

★ **But look out for bandits**

Marco Polo thought that Persia was pleasant, with wealthy towns and cities. But he was terrified by stories of the Karaunas. These bandits used magic to turn day into night, Polo said. Then up to 10,000 horsemen robbed anyone they could find in the dark.

FOLLOWERS OF THE BUDDHA

+ Faith flourishes in remote monasteries

In a state called Tangut, in northwest China, Marco met many **Buddhists**. He noticed that there were statues of Buddha along the road. The Polos also visited monasteries where up to 2,000 monks lived together. They wore robes of black and blue, and ate only bran and water. They spent most of their time praying, and slept on thin, uncomfortable mats. Polo said, "They lead a harder life than any men in the world."

Buddha

Marco Polo called Buddhists idolators, or people who worshiped statues, or idols. But he admired the discipline of the Buddhist way of life.

BUY, BUY, BUY!

- Merchants on the Silk Road
- Fortunes to be made

The Silk Road spread across Asia. Many merchants traveled along parts of it. Cities such as Samarkand, in Uzbekistan, where merchants met to trade, had people of many races. Although goods traveled long distances, most merchants made only short journeys before selling their goods. It was rare to travel the whole route, like the Polos.

The Places I've Seen

As Kublai Khan's ambassador, Marco Polo visited many cities and regions throughout the Mongol empire. He reported on their wonders to the Khan—but his accounts were not always reliable.

THE CITY OF THE SANDS

+ Buddhist center

At the end of their journey to China, the Polos passed Dunhuang. It was one of the most eastern towns on the Silk Road. Huge sand dunes towered nearby. When the wind blew across the dunes, the grains of sand made an eerie noise like singing. Dunhuang was a Buddhist center. It had many temples full of paintings and statues of Buddha.

The Crocodiles of Karagian

- Explorer's report impresses emperor
- European traveler hired as... traveler

When Polo visited a city in China named Karagian, he wrote about the crocodiles, which he mistook for a type of snake. His report was otherwise so accurate that Kublai Khan asked him to travel around the empire. He wanted Polo to report on what he found so Kublai would know what was going on.

AMAZING CITY!

★ **More bridges than Venice!**

★ **A paradise on Earth**

Polo visited many cities but his favorite was Kinsai, now known as Hangzhou in eastern China. Back then, Polo said it had 3,000 public baths and 12,000 bridges. Arab and Persian trading ships sailed in and out of the city. The people were so peaceful they had no weapons. They enjoyed themselves by sailing on a lake, and held celebrations in pavilions built on two small islands near the city.

Did you know?

In what is now Bangladesh, Marco said that he saw magicians and oxen as tall as elephants.

> " It is the greatest city in the world, where so many pleasures may be found that one fancies himself to be in Paradise."
>
> *Marco Polo describes Kinsai.*

My Explorer Journal

★ **Marco Polo described some places that were so unbelievable they were probably not real. Perhaps he wanted to entertain and impress the Khan. Imagine your own city and write a letter to describe some of its wonders.**

Blooming Burmese!

☛ **Gold glows in their mouths!**

One place Polo visited was Burma (now Myanmar). He reported that people there covered their teeth with gold. The men tattooed stripes on their arms and legs. Polo saw a king's tomb made of gold, and silver pagodas, or towers, and met a living king who had 400 wives.

I Love Nature

Marco Polo described so many animals it is difficult to tell which are real and which are imaginary. For example, he described elephants—but he also said he had seen a unicorn!

TRAVEL UPDATE

Tigers on the Loose

★ In Tibet, which was overrun by tigers, Marco Polo described a useful trick. At night, they would tie bamboo canes in bundles and place them around their camp. They would set them on fire, and the heat would make the canes explode. Wild animals were frightened away by the popping noise.

Horns

Polo reported that people used the sheep's horns to shape into bowls for drinking—or to construct pens to hold other sheep.

MOUNTAIN SHEEP

★ **Explorer spots new species**

★ **Sheep hunted widely**

In the highlands of what is now Afghanistan, Marco Polo saw huge flocks of up to 600 wild sheep. The sheep were plump and good climbers, and when they were older they had long, spiraled horns. The local people hunted them with bows and arrows for their meat and wool. Today the animals' official name is *Ovis ammon polii*, or Marco Polo sheep.

MISTAKEN IDENTITY

+ A serpent with legs? Really?

When he saw crocodiles, Polo thought they were a type of **adder** with small legs but no feet. He said they were "very hideous" and were big enough to swallow a man whole. But he also described how hunters trapped crocodiles to use their organs for medicine and to eat their flesh.

My Explorer Journal

★ **Marco Polo mistakenly thought crocodiles were a type of snake. Using the photo on this page, write a detailed description of a crocodile for someone who has not seen one.**

WORMS WORTH A FORTUNE

★ **Explorer learns secrets of silk**

When Marco Polo arrived in China, the Italians had just started producing silk. In China, it had been made for over 4,000 years. Marco saw silkworms feeding on mulberry leaves as they spun their fine cocoons. Then the cocoons were boiled in water, and the silk was carefully unwound to use to make luxury textiles.

BEAST OF BURDEN

- Bactrian camel is the best
- Suitable for hot or cold conditions

The best animals for carrying goods across the deserts were camels. They could go for days without water. But Bactrian camels were also very useful in the cold mountains, because they were insulated by fur. When camels were gathered into a caravan, the first animal was often tied to a donkey, which led the way.

Fortune Hunting

The Polos were traders. They set out for Asia to buy goods they could bring back and sell. By entering the service of the Khan, they became more wealthy than they could ever have dreamed.

BIZARRE BAZAARS

- World's richest cities
- Anything for sale!

The Silk Road passed through many cities and **bazaars** where merchants traded for fresh animals, supplies, and other goods. They sold goods from covered stalls and tents. Chinese goods included cinnamon, rhubarb, furs, tea, ceramics, weapons, and mirrors.

Did you know?

One of the reasons spices were so valuable in Europe was that they gave a variety of flavor to a boring diet and disguised food that could be a bit rotten.

IN THE SERVICE OF THE KHAN

+ Living like a king (nearly!)

Polo's first report to the Khan was so detailed that the emperor made Marco a regional ambassador. Marco would be the Khan's official representative in other lands—and he would give Kublai reports on everything he saw on his travels. That meant Marco lived in the Khan's palace as a wealthy man.

RICHES OF ASIA

★ **Silk, spices, and stones**

★ **Asian goods are all the rage**

Although silk gave its name to the trade route, other goods were also highly valued. Europeans paid high prices for spices such as pepper and cinnamon. They helped disguise the taste of stale food. In Afghanistan they also mined a blue stone, called lapis lazuli, which was used for jewelry.

SILKY SMOOTH

★ **High fashion in Europe**

Silk was in great demand among Europe's wealthiest people. It was light and smooth, and very comfortable to wear. But the Europeans had only just begun to produce silk, so they relied on importing the cloth from China. Silk production, called sericulture, was big business there. It was so important in China that myths said that the gods had taught one of the first Chinese rulers the secret of how to make silk.

PORTABLE WEALTH

☛ **Polos hide jewels in their clothes**

When the Polos set out to take the Mongol princess Kokachin to be married in Persia, Kublai Khan provided boats. He gave them many rubies and other valuable jewels. The Polos sewed them into their clothes. This was how travelers often protected their possessions from being stolen at a time when few garments had pockets. Kublai Khan also paid the three men expenses for their ten years' service. They had become wealthy men.

This Isn't What It Said in the Brochure!

Many parts of Marco Polo's journey were quite easy. Merchants traveled the Silk Road all the time. But there were times when the Polos faced such dangers that Marco wondered if it was all worthwhile.

BANDITS IN THE SAND

☞ **Unwary travelers attacked**

Marco Polo claimed that he narrowly escaped being captured by the Karaunas bandits. Polo reported that the Karaunas captured and sold some of his companions as slaves; they executed others.

☁ Weather Forecast

GETTING COLDER

As they traveled east, the Polos faced colder temperatures. They crossed Badakshan, in what is now Afghanistan. People there mined rubies, lapis lazuli, and sapphires. Marco fell sick, but was cured by the clean air of the Pamir Mountains in South-Central Asia.

Did you know?

In Persia, Polo complained that it was so cold it was impossible for the travelers to get warm, no matter how many layers of clothes they put on.

TRAVEL UPDATE

Lost in the Sands

★ The Silk Road crossed the Gobi Desert. There were some wells but no food, so all supplies had to be carried. Travelers could easily become lost, tricked into following **mirages** or distracted by passing caravans. At night, eerie howls and drumming had to be ignored as the traveler's mind would play tricks.

Desert

Polo said that travelers in the desert heard voices call their names and followed them into the sand, where they disappeared. He blamed this on evil spirits.

LEAKY BOATS

★ **I'm not sailing in that!**

Marco refused to sail from Persia to India. He claimed that many boats sank because they were stitched together with thread made from coconut husks.

SEA MONSTERS

+ **Polo fears attacks on boat**

Sea travel in the 1200s was often risky. When the Polos sailed from China, Marco feared that a giant whale might surface underneath the ship and tip it over. In fact, he said that of the 600 people who left China, only 18 survived the 18-month voyage to Persia. He did not say what happened to the others: they probably died of disease or starvation.

End of the Road

The Polos returned to Venice in 1295, after being away for 24 years. But Marco still had more adventures to come, and he later became one of the most famous authors in the world.

AUTHOR AT WORK

- Marco Polo spills the beans
- Describes a whole new world

In prison, Marco described his adventures to another captive, Rustichello da Pisa. Rustichello's job outside prison was writing legal documents. He wrote down Polo's stories. He added some stories of his own and some general gossip about China. Handwritten **manuscripts** of the book spread around Europe. Later, it was printed, and even more people read it.

Family

Marco was freed in 1299. He married a merchant's daughter named Donata. They had three daughters: Bellela, Moretta, and Fantina. Marco died in Venice in 1323.

IMPRISONED!

★ Explorer fights for Venice

★ Captured and thrown in prison

When Marco Polo got home, Venice was at war with Genoa, another Italian trading city. Marco used some of his wealth to buy a warship, called a galley. But when he sailed to fight for Venice he was captured by the Genoese. They threw him into prison.

CHANGING TITLES

+ Author's account all lies: Shocking Claim

Marco Polo's book was the first real information Europeans had about China from someone who had actually been there. It had various titles. It was called *Description of the World* or *Book of the Marvels of the World*. Today, the book is usually known in English as *The Travels of Marco Polo*.

My Explorer Journal

★ **People criticized Marco Polo for telling lies about Asia in his book. Give reasons why you think he was telling the truth or making things up. Use details from this book in your answer.**

I have not told the half of what I saw."
Marco Polo's reply to those who criticized his account

INSPIRING EUROPE

☛ **Marco Polo sets the tone**

☛ **Explorers follow Polos' footsteps**

Not everyone doubted Polo's stories about Asia. Many merchants became convinced that Asia had valuable goods to trade. More Europeans began to head east along the Silk Road. These travelers did not only visit China, they also explored India and Muscovy (present-day Russia). As contacts grew, Europeans learned more and more about Asia and how people there lived.

Did you know?

Christopher Columbus made many notes on his copy of Marco Polo's book. The book encouraged him to set out in 1492 to sail west to reach China. Instead, he landed in America.

GLOSSARY

adder A venomous snake

astrolabe An early navigational instrument used to measure the height of the sun or other celestial bodies above the horizon

astronomy The science of heavenly bodies

bazaars Markets where merchants do business from temporary stalls

Buddhists People who follow the teachings of Buddha

caravan A group of traders traveling together on animals across a desert

carrack A large merchant sailing ship with over 1,000 tons (900 metric tons) of storage, with the ability to remain steady in rough waters

equator An imaginary line that runs around the middle of Earth

friars Members of a group of religious men

junks Traditional sailing ships used by the Chinese

mangonels Large, wheeled catapults used to throw stones in warfare

manuscripts Documents written out in handwriting

merchants People who buy and sell large quantities of goods, often involving overseas trade

Middle Ages The period in European history lasting from the 5th to the 15th century

mirages In a desert, illusions of water in a dry area

Muslims People who observe the Islamic religion

nomads People who travel from place to place and have no permanent home

pilots Sailors who steer a vessel, often in dangerous waters

quadrant An instrument for navigation in the shape of a quarter–circle

raided Attacked or suddenly invaded

spices Plants such as pepper or cinnamon that are used to flavor food

unicorns Legendary animals similar to a horse with a single, long horn on their foreheads

yurts Round, flat-roofed tents made from animal skins

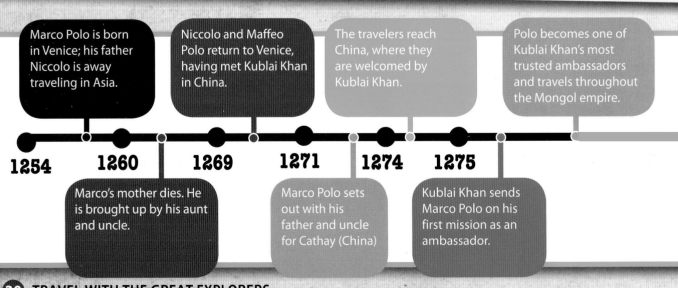

Marco Polo is born in Venice; his father Niccolo is away traveling in Asia.

Niccolo and Maffeo Polo return to Venice, having met Kublai Khan in China.

The travelers reach China, where they are welcomed by Kublai Khan.

Polo becomes one of Kublai Khan's most trusted ambassadors and travels throughout the Mongol empire.

1254 **1260** **1269** **1271** **1274** **1275**

Marco's mother dies. He is brought up by his aunt and uncle.

Marco Polo sets out with his father and uncle for Cathay (China)

Kublai Khan sends Marco Polo on his first mission as an ambassador.

ON THE WEB

www.enchantedlearning.com/explorers/page/p/polo.shtml
Guide to Marco Polo's life at Enchanted Learning.

www.silk-road.com/artl/marcopolo.shtml
A guide to Marco's travels on the Silk Road and in East Asia.

history.howstuffworks.com/historical-figures/who-was-marco-polo.htm
How Stuff Works biography of Marco Polo.

www.softschools.com/timelines/marco_polo_timeline/23/
Timeline of Marco's life and achievements from SoftSchools.com.

BOOKS

Bankston, John. *Marco Polo* (Junior Biographies from Ancient Civilizations). Mitchell Lane Publishers, 2013.

Feinstein, Stephen. *Marco Polo: Amazing Adventures in China* (Great Explorers of the World). Enslow Publishers Inc, 2009.

Holub, Joan, and John O'Brien. *Who Was Marco Polo?* (Who was...?) Grosset and Dunlap, 2007.

Morley, Jacqueline. *You Wouldn't Want to Explore with Marco Polo!: A Really Long Trip You'd Rather Not Take.* Franklin Watts, 2009.

Ollhoff, Jim. *Marco Polo* (Great Explorers). Abdo and Daughters, 2013.

Zelenyj, Alexander. *Marco Polo: Overland to China* (In the Footsteps of Explorers). Crabtree Publishing Company, 2006.

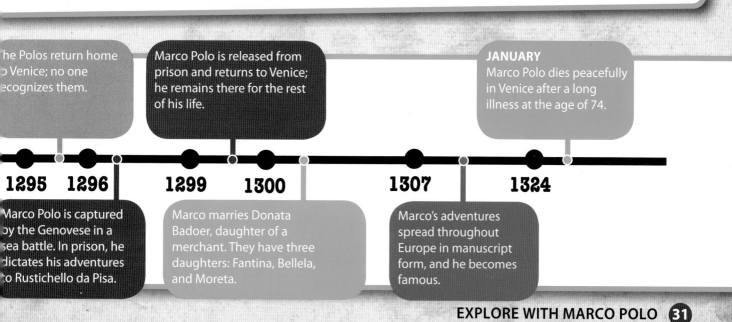

The Polos return home to Venice; no one recognizes them.

Marco Polo is released from prison and returns to Venice; he remains there for the rest of his life.

JANUARY
Marco Polo dies peacefully in Venice after a long illness at the age of 74.

1295 **1296** **1299** **1300** **1307** **1324**

Marco Polo is captured by the Genovese in a sea battle. In prison, he dictates his adventures to Rustichello da Pisa.

Marco marries Donata Badoer, daughter of a merchant. They have three daughters: Fantina, Bellela, and Moreta.

Marco's adventures spread throughout Europe in manuscript form, and he becomes famous.

INDEX